All About

SHARKS!

A SEA WORLD BOOK ™

Published by

THIRD STORY BOOKS™

955 Connecticut Avenue, Suite 1302

Bridgeport, Connecticut 06607

ISBN 1 - 884506 - 10 - 0

Distributed to the trade by

Andrews & McMeel

4900 Main Street

Kansas City, Missouri 64112

Library of Congress Catalog Card Number: 93-61829

Printed in Singapore

All About
SHARKS!

Written by Jane Resnick

FEATURING Sea World. PHOTOGRAPHY

THIRD™ STORY BOOKS

Surprising Sharks

Say shark and only one picture comes to mind — it's big, it's gray, it looks like a lean, mean submarine. Not necessarily so. There are more than 350 different types of sharks. The smallest is only nine inches. The largest, the whale shark, can be as long as 45 feet and weigh 40,000 pounds.

A sand tiger shark looks like what most people think a shark should look like. Sand tigers can be found at Sea World.

Sharks existed about 400 million years ago. That's 200 million years before dinosaurs made their appearance. Sharks continued to evolve until about 100 million years ago, and haven't changed all that much since.

Sharks are one of the world's best survivors.

The hammerhead shark is one of the last to evolve, which may explain why it is more social than most sharks.

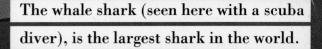

The whale shark (seen here with a scuba diver), is the largest shark in the world.

The One and Only

All sharks have skeletons of *cartilage*, not bone, like most fish. Cartilage is lighter and more flexible. Sharks have scales, called *denticles*, that are similar to tiny sharp teeth and are rough and jagged and feel like sandpaper.

Sharks have five different kinds of fins. They are: caudal fins, anal fins, dorsal fins, pelvic fins and pectoral fins.

The fin at the back is the caudal fin. This blacktip shark has two dorsal fins on top and an anal fin underneath just in front of the caudal fin.

A shark can use electricity to find food! All living creatures give off small electrical signals. A shark can sense even the weakest electrical field by use of tiny receptors on its head called the "ampullae of Lorenzini."

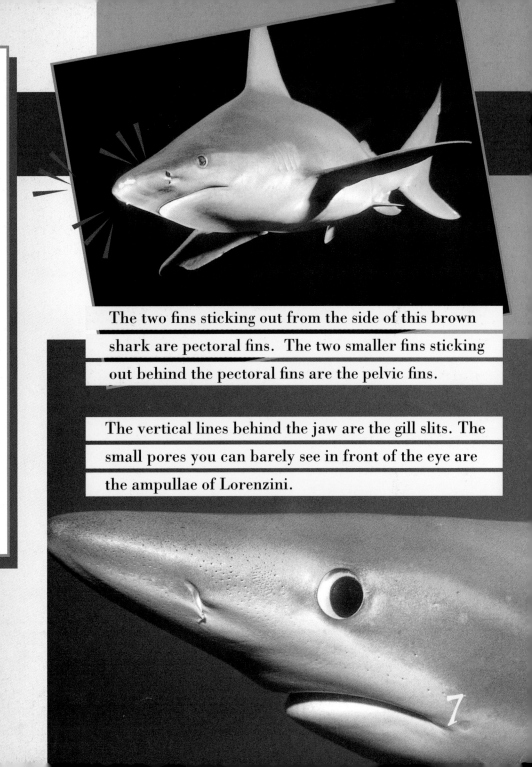

The two fins sticking out from the side of this brown shark are pectoral fins. The two smaller fins sticking out behind the pectoral fins are the pelvic fins.

The vertical lines behind the jaw are the gill slits. The small pores you can barely see in front of the eye are the ampullae of Lorenzini.

7

Super Senses

Nostrils are located just above the mouth.

Sharks have only an inner ear. Because sound travels faster through water than air, sound is often the first sense a shark uses to locate prey.

The shark's eye is large and well suited to seeing in dim light.

Sharks smell very well. They are well known for their ability to detect minute quantities of substances such as blood in water.

A shark can "feel" the direction of its prey, by using its "lateral line," an organ along the sides of its body that picks up the vibrations of movement in the water.

Sharks use an organ called a lateral line to pick up movement in the water.

Like most sharks, these bonnethead sharks can see well in dim light.

Shark Bite

These teeth were gathered from the floor of a shark exhibit at Sea World.

Sharks have rows and rows of teeth. But they are not set firmly in the jaw. The front teeth are easily lost, but they are replaced by teeth moving up from behind. The sand tiger shark may produce and shed 2,400 teeth in its lifetime.

The type of shark's teeth depends on what it eats. The great white has big teeth—2 1/2 inch triangles, sharp as a blade. Bottom feeders like horn sharks have pointed front teeth for grasping and flat back teeth for crushing.

The lemon shark can replace a tooth in about eight days.

The blue shark's short jaws make for a very powerful bite. This blue is feasting on squid.

Feeding Time

Sharks are not picky eaters but they aren't piggy either. They're carnivores, which means they eat flesh, mostly fishes which they swallow whole. They'll also eat crustaceans, mollusks, marine mammals, and even other sharks. But they only eat when they're hungry, and a good meal can last a shark for a week or more.

The bamboo shark is a ground feeder — it will look for food on the bottom of the ocean.

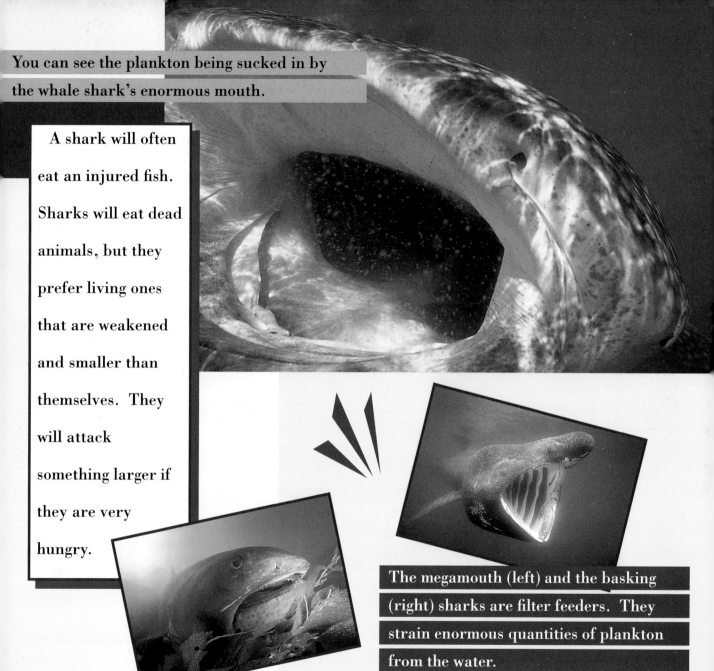

You can see the plankton being sucked in by the whale shark's enormous mouth.

A shark will often eat an injured fish. Sharks will eat dead animals, but they prefer living ones that are weakened and smaller than themselves. They will attack something larger if they are very hungry.

The megamouth (left) and the basking (right) sharks are filter feeders. They strain enormous quantities of plankton from the water.

13

Utensils Not Necessary

The horn shark has front teeth that are pointed for grasping and back teeth that are flat for crushing.

Although some sharks aren't very selective about what they eat, certain sharks eat some foods more than others. Hammerhead sharks eat primarily stingrays, bull sharks prefer other fishes, smooth dogfish sharks like crabs and lobster, and tiger sharks look for sea turtles.

14

The nurse shark uses its thick lips to create suction that can pull its prey from holes or hard-to-get-at places.

Most predatory sharks seize, grasp, and tear food. A shark may circle its prospective prey and may even bump it with its snout or pectoral fins.

The sawfish moves its head from side to side and strikes prey with its long rostrum.

15

A newborn shark is called a pup, but it can take care of itself at birth. Sharks are born in different ways. Some grow inside the mother and are born fully formed. Others come from eggs that are laid in the water in the form of small, odd-shaped cases.

A swell shark hatches from an egg.

Shark pregnancies can take a long time. The lemon shark spends a year developing, and the dogfish takes two years. Sharks that are born fully developed have a good chance of survival.

A Pacific blacktip shark is born fully formed and able to fend for itself at birth.

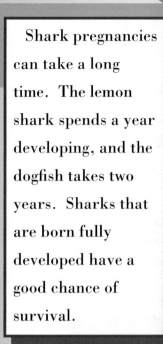

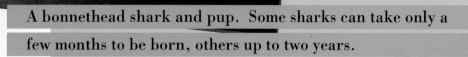

A bonnethead shark and pup. Some sharks can take only a few months to be born, others up to two years.

17

Sharks of Many Colors

The Caribbean reef shark has countershading colors.

Most sharks are countershaded. This is a kind of camouflage that makes sharks hard to see.

A shark might be dark on the top, which makes it hard to see from above looking into the dark ocean. But on the bottom it might be light-shaded to make it hard to see when looking up towards the brightness of the surface.

18

Some sharks are colored to blend in with their surroundings, often the bottom of the ocean. Most stripes and other markings are colors present in young sharks that disappear with age.

The angel shark (above) is hard to see near the bottom of the ocean. The zebra shark (left) keeps its unique markings throughout its life.

19

How Weird! A Ray!

Rays are the shark's cousins. These strange fish are built like a shark that's been ironed flat. Their eyes are on top of their heads and their mouths are on the bottom. The pectoral fins, extending from head to tail, look like giant wings. They belong to an order called batoids which includes stingrays, electric rays, guitarfish, skates, and sawfish. Rays eat the same kinds of food that sharks eat.

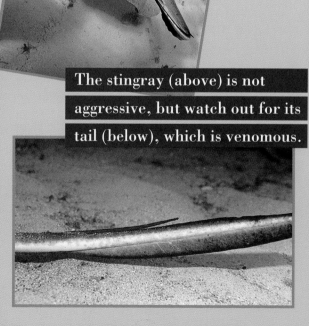

The stingray (above) is not aggressive, but watch out for its tail (below), which is venomous.

Rays are not aggressive, but some are dangerous. The torpedo ray is electric and delivers a stunning shock.

The cow-nosed ray can be found at Sea World.

The manta is the largest of all rays, and can reach a width of over 22 feet.

Little Buddies

A remora fastens itself onto the body of a shark.

Sharks don't have "friends," but they do have something very close to them—you might even say attached. Remoras are fishes with a suction disk on their heads. They fasten themselves to sharks and hitchhike. When sharks attack, remoras dine on the scraps. They "earn their dinner" by eating parasites (worms, leeches and tiny shellfish) that feed on a shark's body.

Pilot fish are companions that stay very close to a shark's head where it is easier for them to swim. Enemies of these small fish stay away as long as they are with their big companions. And pilot fish get a free meal, too, eating the leftovers of a shark attack.

Two remoras hang close to a shark's tail.

Pilot fish swim nearby a whale shark.

23

Are Sharks Endangered?

Sharks can hardly be called endangered—evidence indicates that sharks' ancestors lived on earth 350 to 400 million years ago, and that most of the modern-day shark families had already evolved more than 100 million years ago. There are over 820 species of sharks and batoids — some of which can be seen at Sea World's Shark Encounter (opposite page).

A shark's enemies include other sharks, elephant seals, killer whales, and humans.

Sharks are vulnerable to overfishing. Recreational and commercial shark fishing have increased over the years because there is a demand for shark products. Many sharks are also caught in nets by mistake.

Shark Attack

It's good to know that humans are not a natural food for sharks. But a shark can easily mistake a human for natural prey, and attack anyway. This is probably true even of the great white shark, which was featured in the movie *Jaws*. At the surface, a swimmer's silhouette resembles that of a sea lion. Great whites eat sea lions, and it is doubtful that it can tell the difference between sea lions and humans.

More people are killed by bee stings than shark bites. And swimmers who are attacked by sharks are far outnumbered by those killed in automobile accidents on their way to the beach.

Sharks like the sand tiger (above) and the great white (facing page), are not natural enemies of man. California has one of the highest rates of great white shark attacks in the world, yet on the average only one person is killed by a great white there every eight years.

27

Sea World Sharks

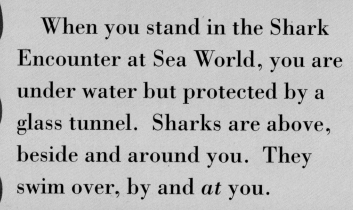

Sand tiger sharks at Sea World's Shark Encounter.

When you stand in the Shark Encounter at Sea World, you are under water but protected by a glass tunnel. Sharks are above, beside and around you. They swim over, by and *at* you.

Because some sharks prey on other sharks, they live in pools according to size. The huge exhibit that surrounds you at Sea World is the place to meet big sharks eyeball to eyeball.

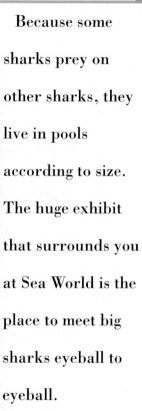

Nose-to-nose with sharks the safe way.

An educational tour through the tunnel at Shark Encounter.

29

Fascinating Facts

Just When You Thought it was Safe to go Back Into the Water. Sharks are thought of as ocean fish, but the bull shark and the Ganges shark can also be found in fresh water.

Ride 'Em Cowboy. In Australia, a country where fishermen can be cowboys too, a great white shark weighing 3,000 pounds was once caught by lasso.

Watch Out! The bull, the tiger, and the great white have been blamed for most attacks on humans.

What's This? The megamouth shark is 15-17 feet long and nobody had ever seen one until 1976 when one was caught by mistake.

Going to Extremes. The largest shark ever recorded is also the largest fish in the whole world. It's a whale shark, 45 feet long and weighing over 40,000 pounds! The smallest shark is about 44 feet shorter than the largest. The spined pygmy only grows to about nine inches.

Glossary

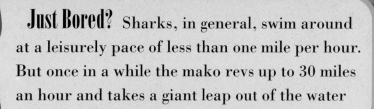

Just Bored? Sharks, in general, swim around at a leisurely pace of less than one mile per hour. But once in a while the mako revs up to 30 miles an hour and takes a giant leap out of the water

Camouflage. A type of disguise or concealment.

Carnivore. An animal that eats meat or fish.

Crustacean. A kind of sea animal with a crusty outer skeleton that includes lobsters, shrimps, crabs, wood lice, water fleas, and barnacles.

Elephant seal. One of two very large seals found either in Pacific coastal waters from southern Alaska to California, or in coastal waters of the antarctic.

Order. A way of grouping plants or animals into categories.

Parasite. Any creature that feeds on another. Worms and leeches, for example, that are found on sharks, are parasites.

Plankton. Plants and animals of the sea, some of which are so small they can only be seen with a microscope.

Pup. The name for a baby shark.

The Marathoner. The blue shark is a long distance swimmer. One has a recorded journey of close to 4,000 miles.

Sea World®

"For in the end we will conserve only what we love.
We will love only what we understand.
And we will understand only what we are taught."

Baba Dioum — noted Central African Naturalist

Since the first Sea World opened in 1964, more than 160 million people have experienced first-hand the majesty and mystery of marine life. Sea World parks have been leaders in building public understanding and appreciation for killer whales, dolphins, and a vast variety of other sea creatures.

Through its work in animal rescue and rehabilitation, breeding, animal care, research and education, Sea World demonstrates a strong commitment to the preservation of marine life and the environment.

Sea World provides all its animals with the highest-quality care including state-of-the-art facilities and stimulating positive reinforcement training programs. Each park employs full-time veterinarians, trainers, biologists and other animal care experts to provide 24-hour care. Through close relationships with these animals — relationships that are built on trust — Sea World's animal care experts are able to monitor their health every day to ensure their well-being. In short, all animals residing at Sea World are treated with respect, love and care.

If you would like more information about Sea World books, please write to us. We'd like to hear from you.

THIRD STORY BOOKS
955 Connecticut Avenue, Suite 1302
Bridgeport, CT 06607